THE BIG BOOK OF SEA MONSTERS

(SCARY LOOKING SEA ANIMALS)

SPEEDY PUBLISHING

Speedy Publishing LLC
40 E. Main St. #1156
Newark, DE 19711
www.speedypublishing.com

Copyright 2015

All Rights reserved. No part of this book may be reproduced or used in any way or form or by any means whether electronic or mechanical, this means that you cannot record or photocopy any material ideas or tips that are provided in this book

The sea is famous for such bizarre wildlife.

Here are some of the scary looking sea animals in this world.

STARGAZER FISH

have mouth, nostrils, and eyes set high in the head. Stargazer fish bury itself in the sand of the area in which they lay their trap and will leave only their eyes unburied.

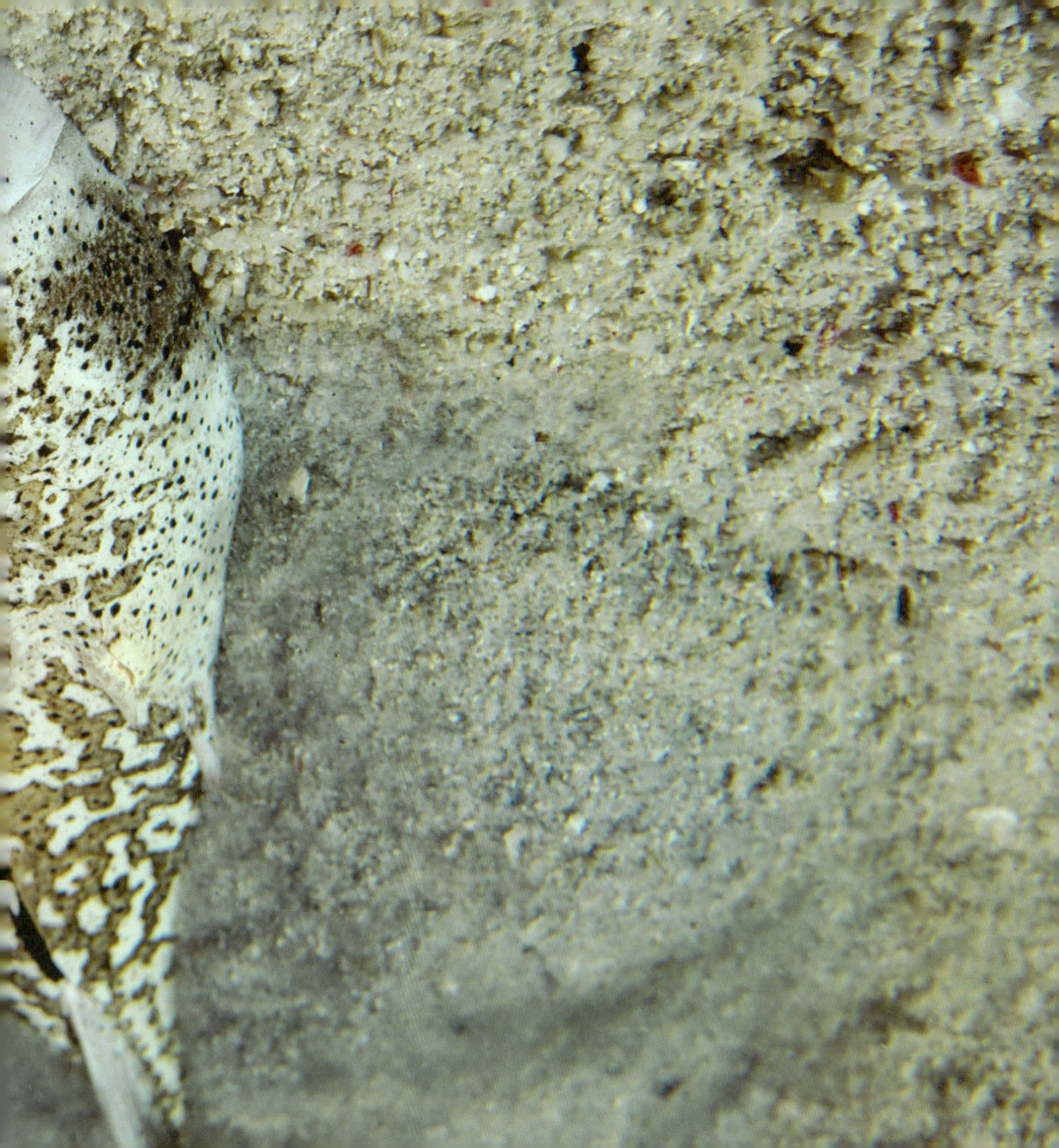

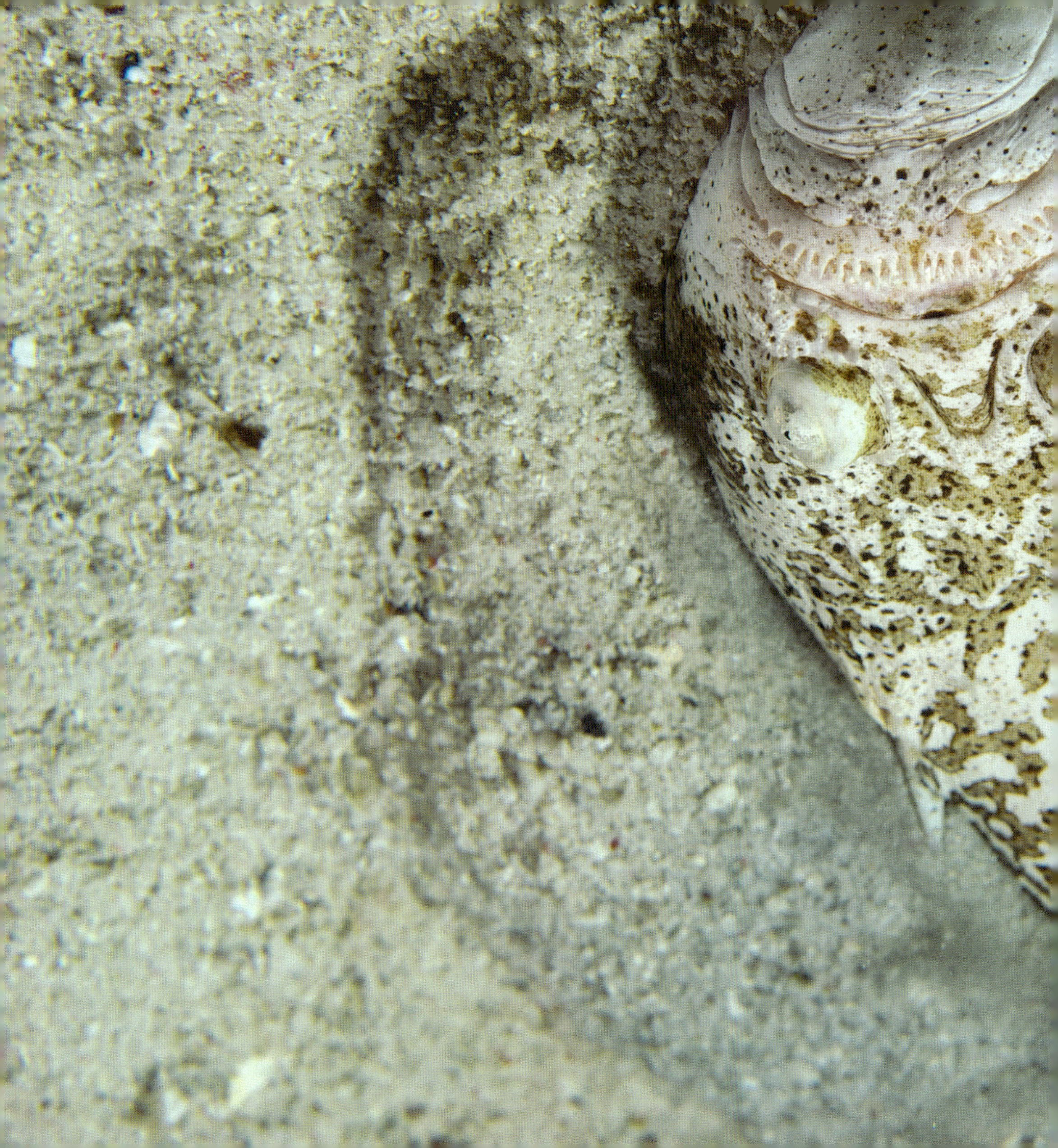

BROADCLUB CUTTLEFISH

is related to squid, octopus and chambered nautilus. Cuttlefish use color to communicate warnings, courtship displays, mood changes or for camouflage.

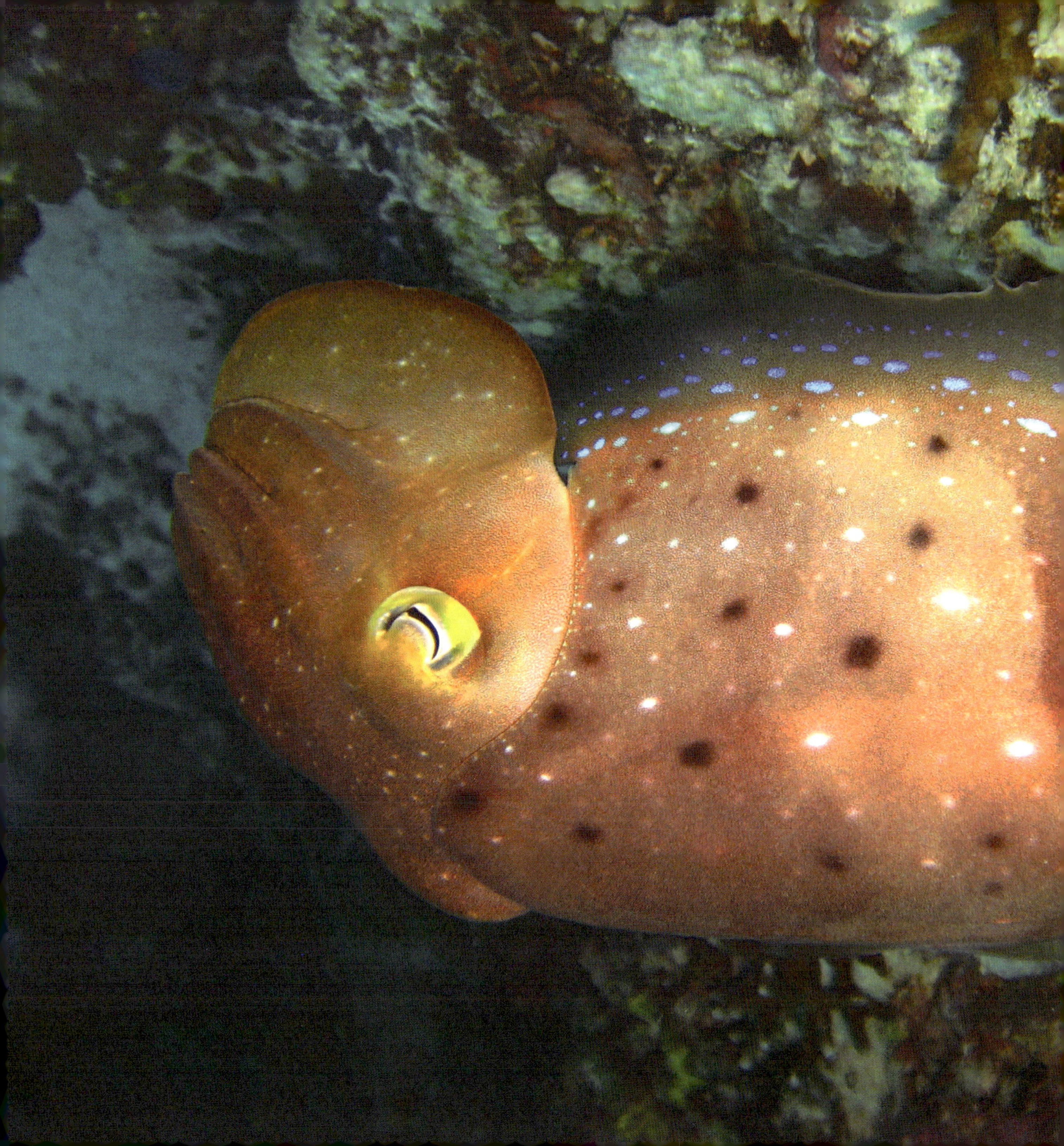

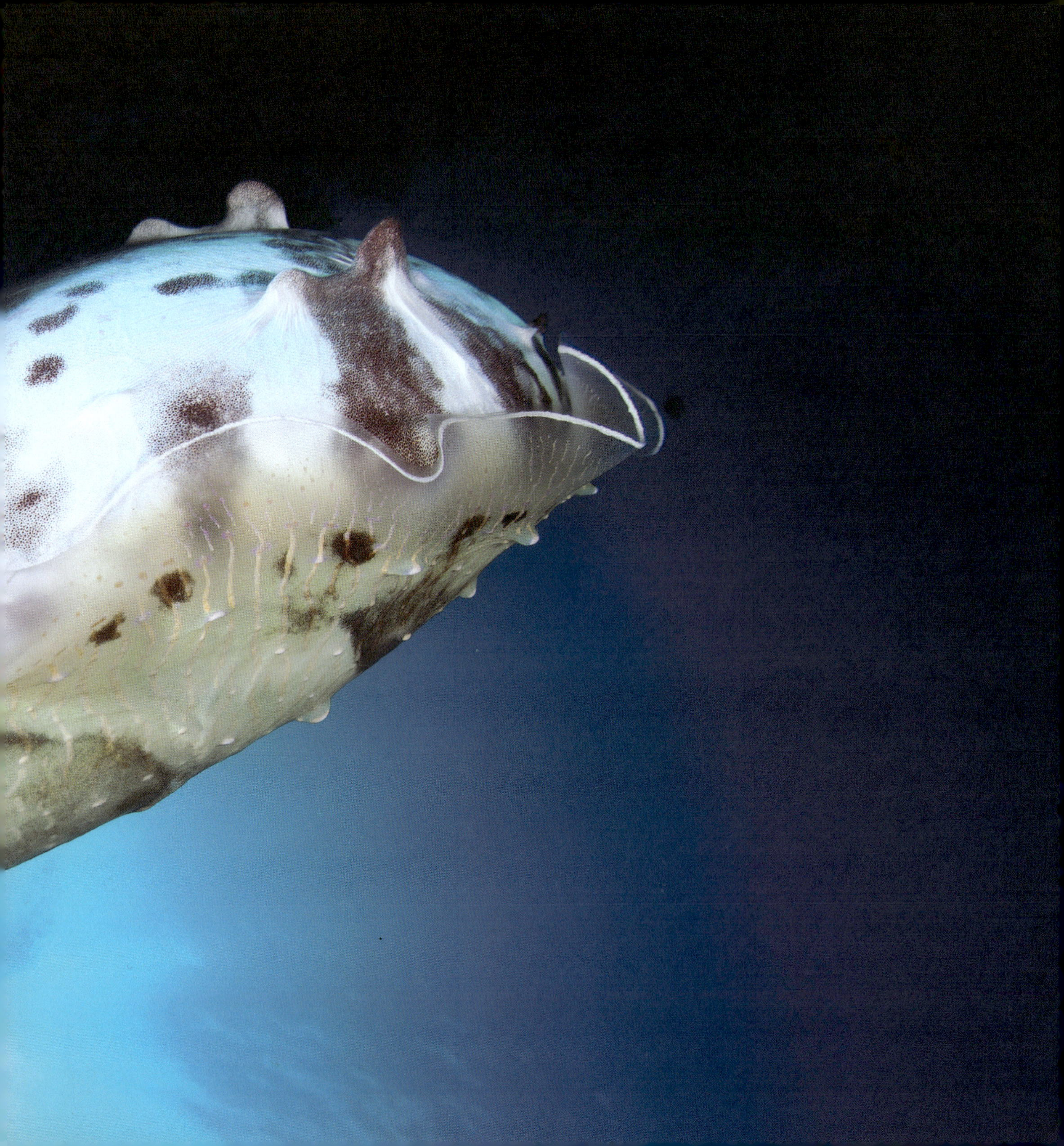

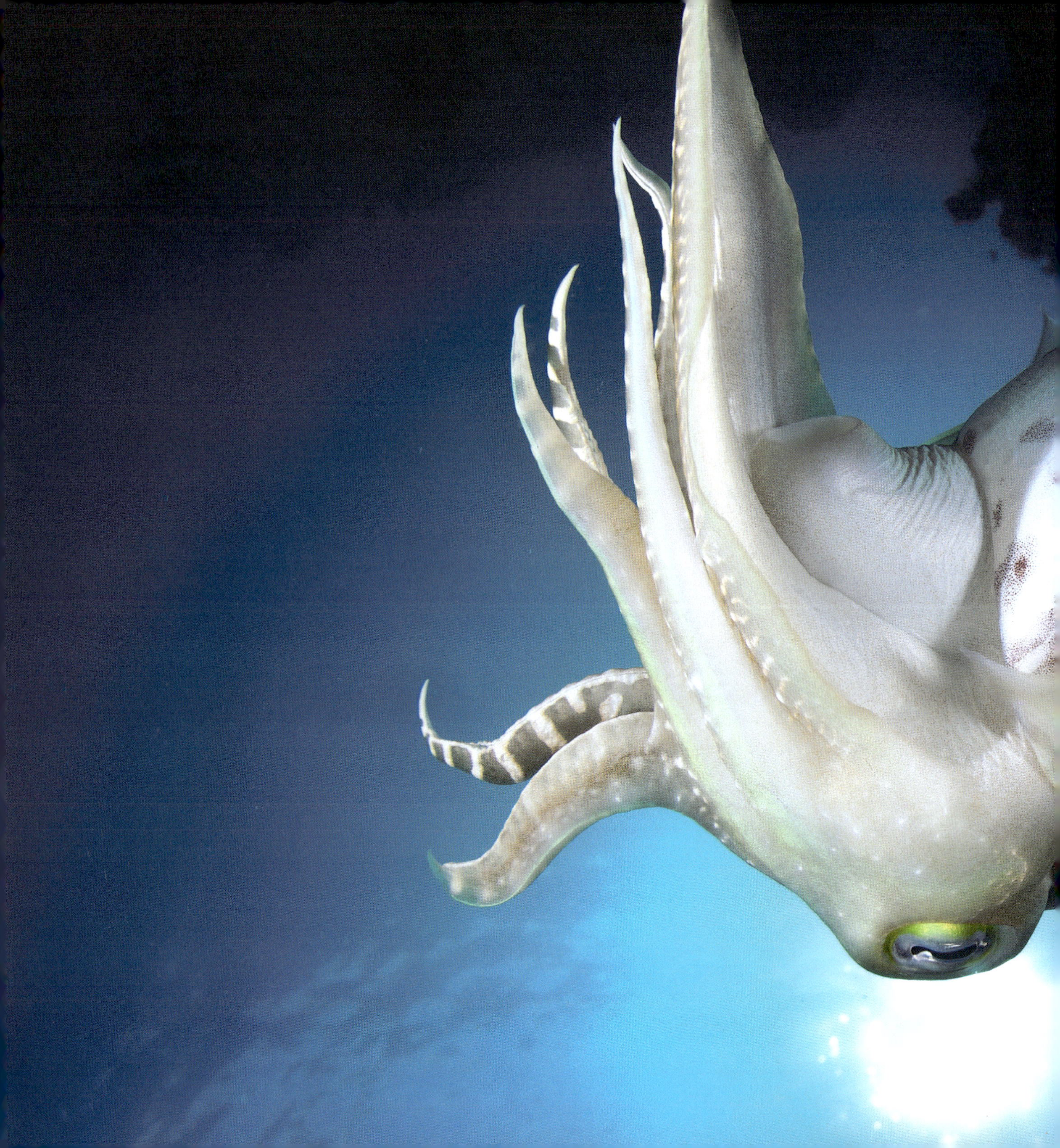

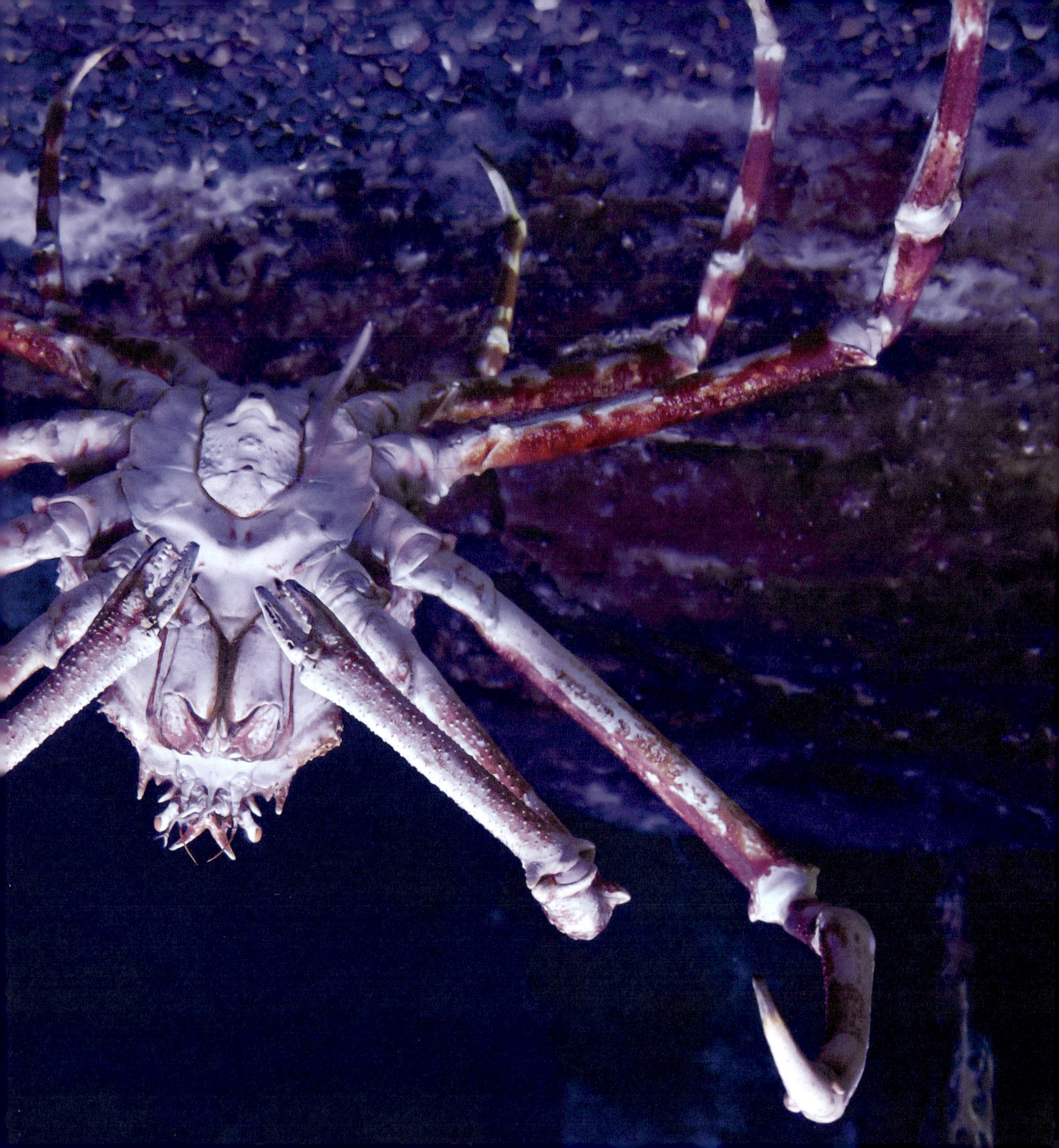

GIANT JAPANESE SPIDER CRAB

has the greatest leg span of any arthropod reaching 12 feet from claw to claw. The Japanese Spider Crab can be found in the waters of Japan.

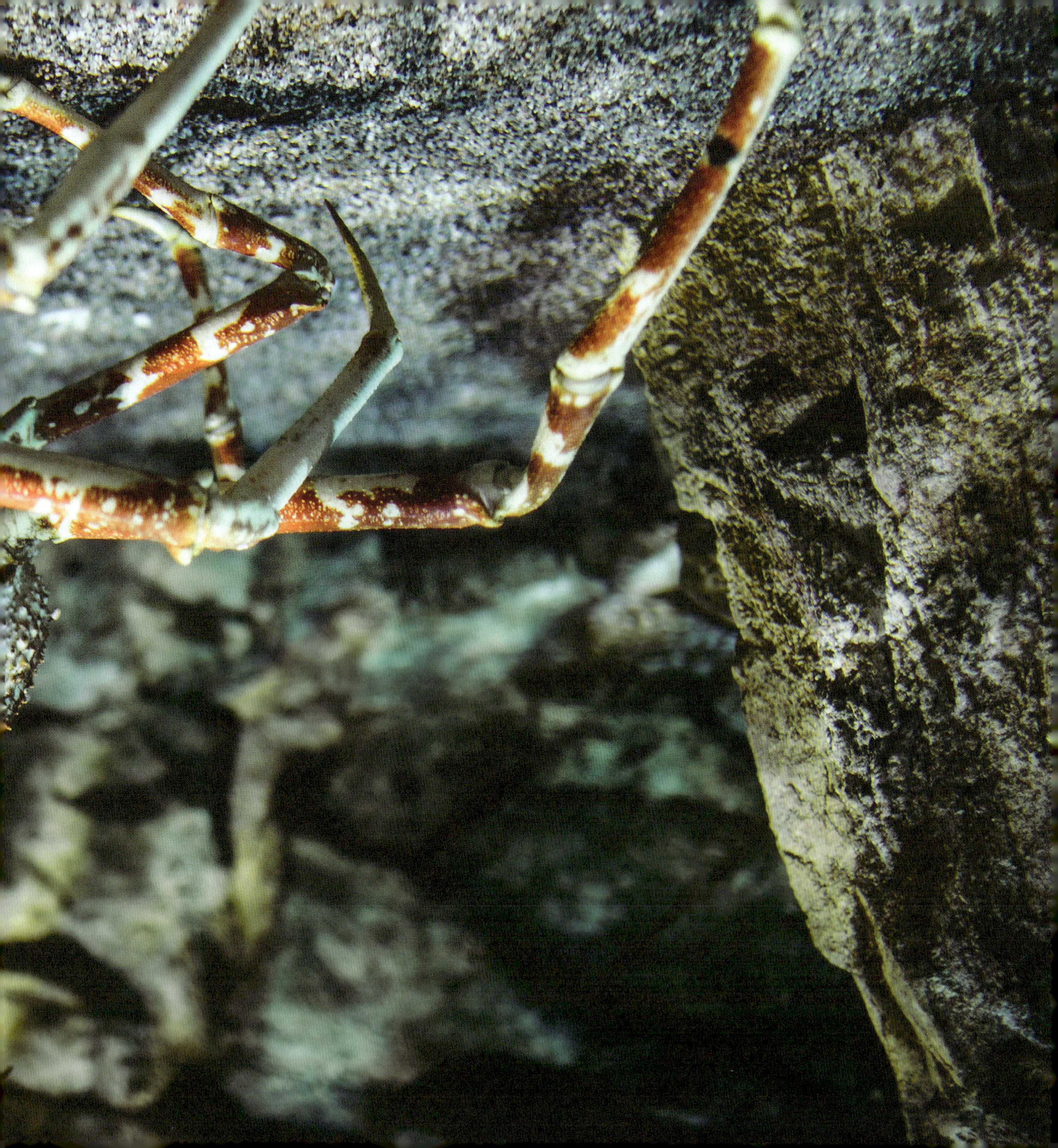

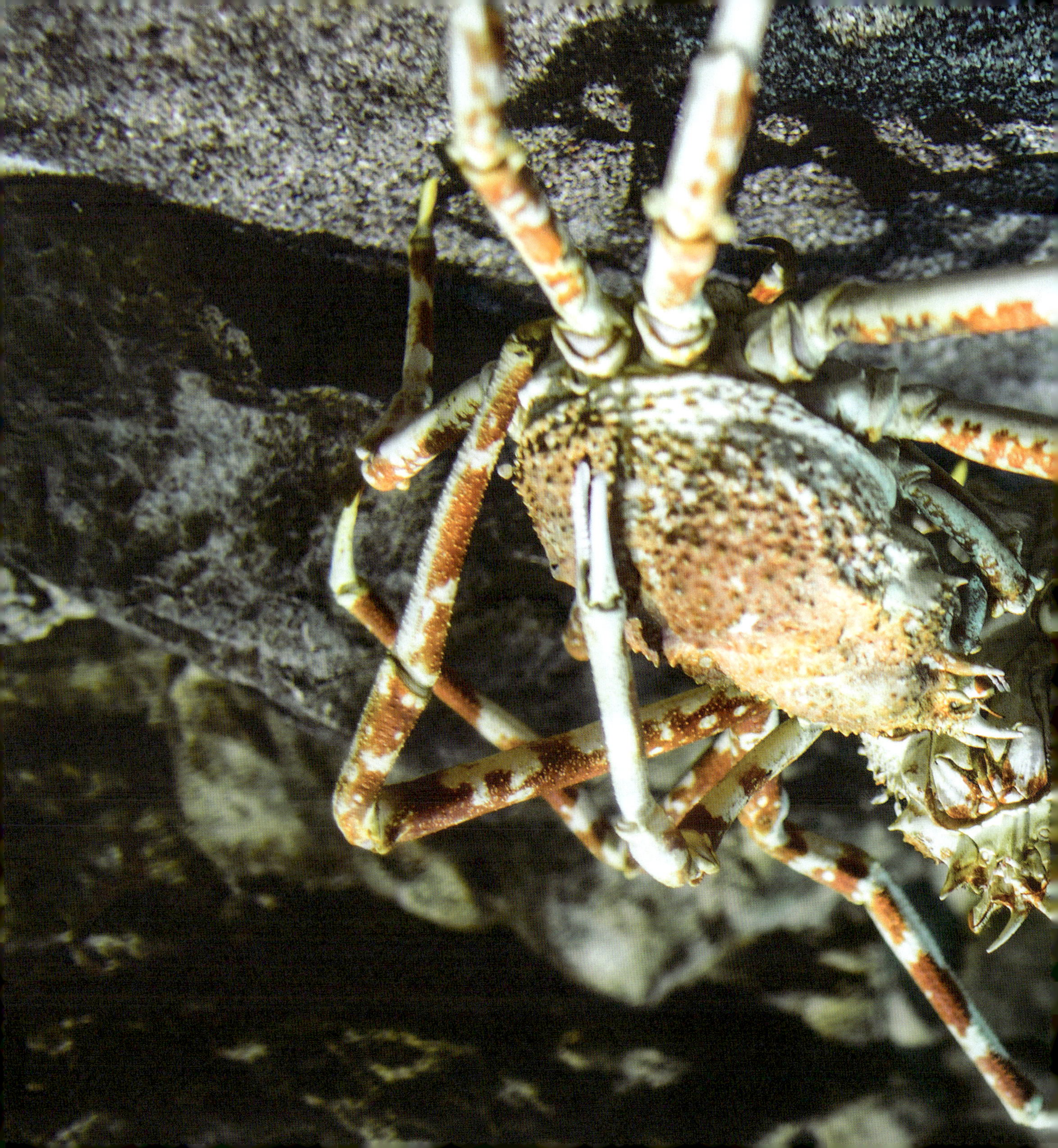

OCEAN SUNFISH

is the largest bony fish species. Ocean sunfish can grow as much as 5,000 pounds. Ocean sunfish are found in temperate and tropical oceans around the world.

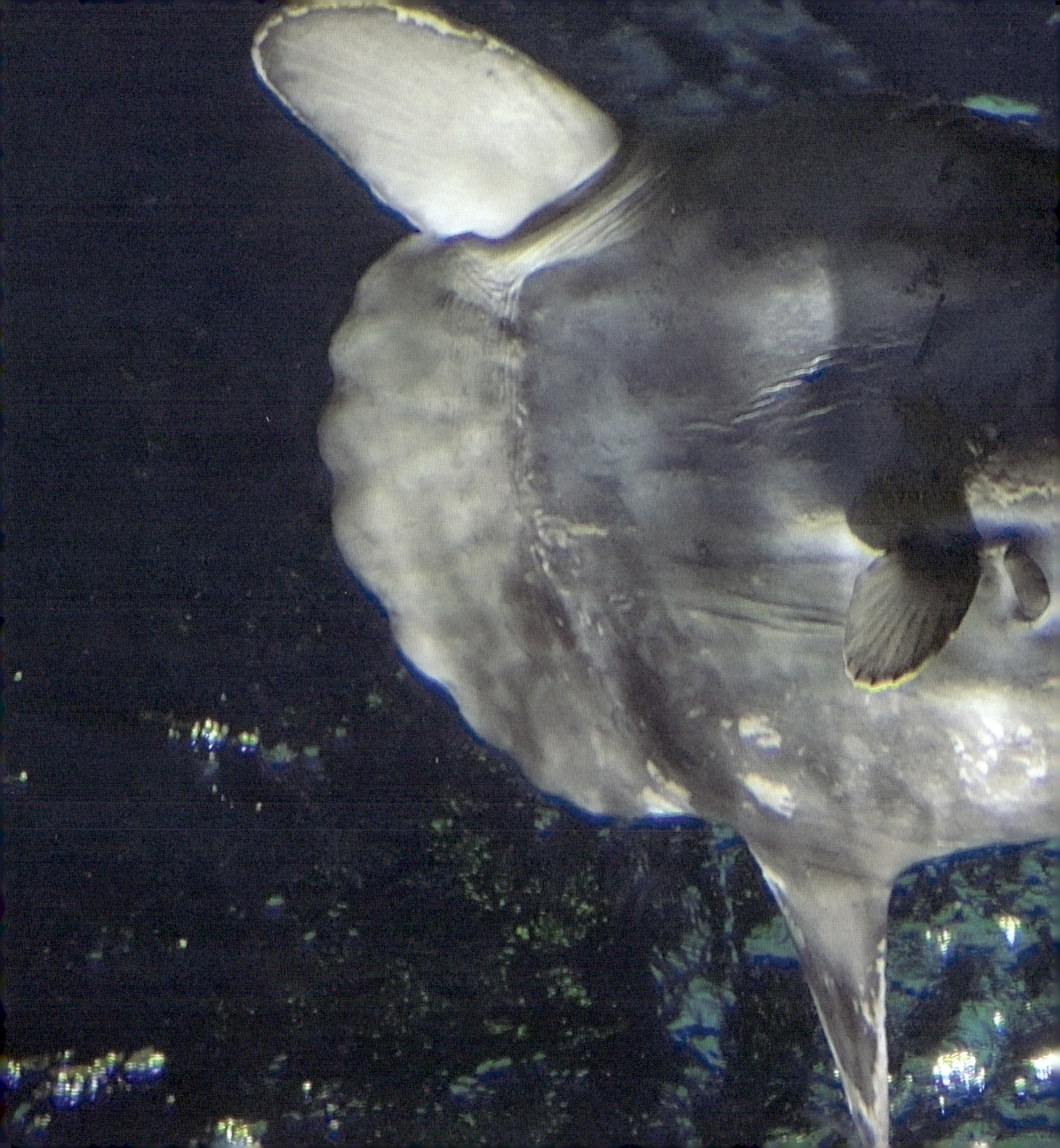

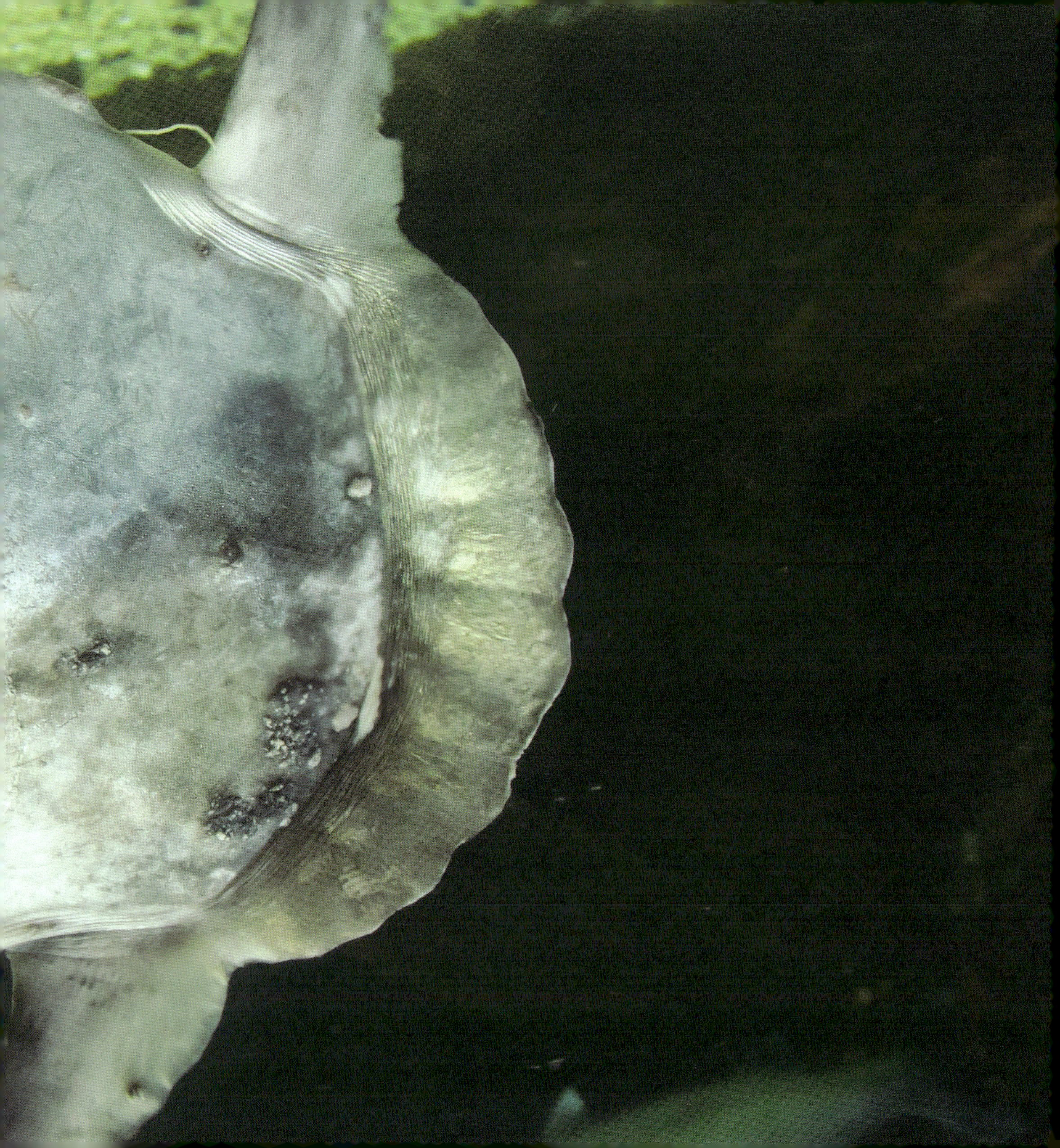

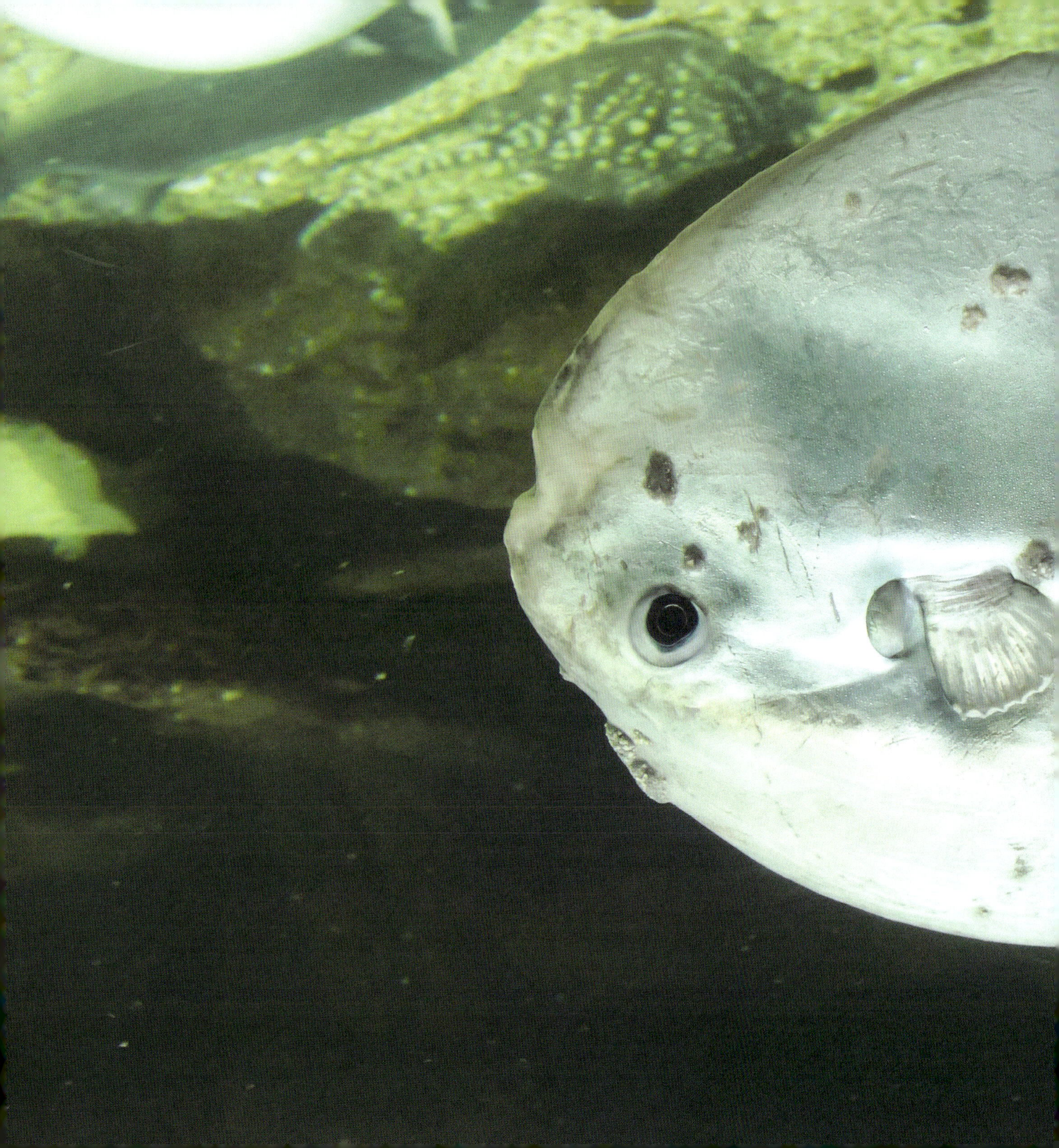

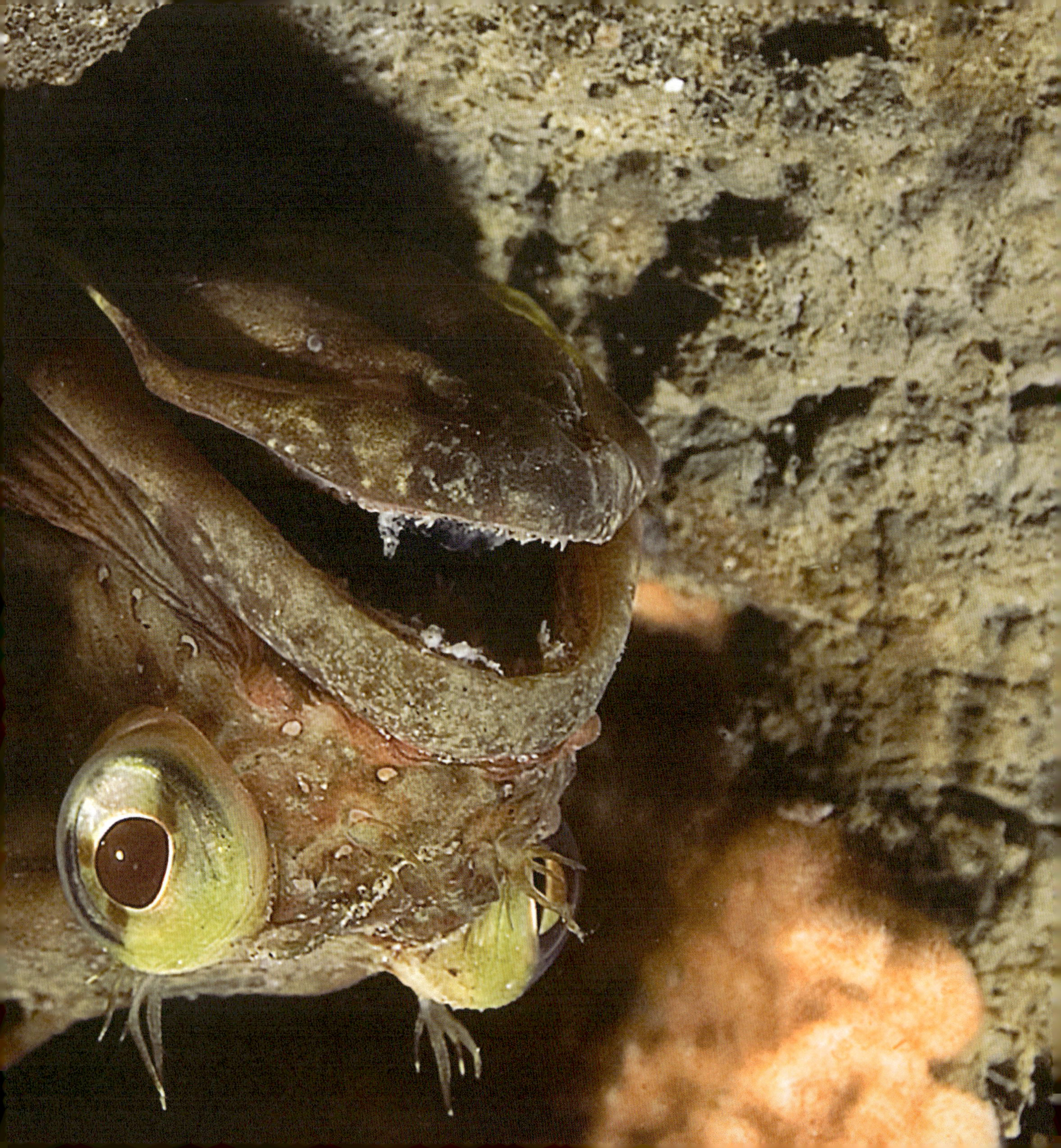

SARCASTIC FRINGEHEAD

is a ferocious fish which has a large mouth and aggressive territorial behavior. Sarcastic fringehead have extremely sharp teeth.

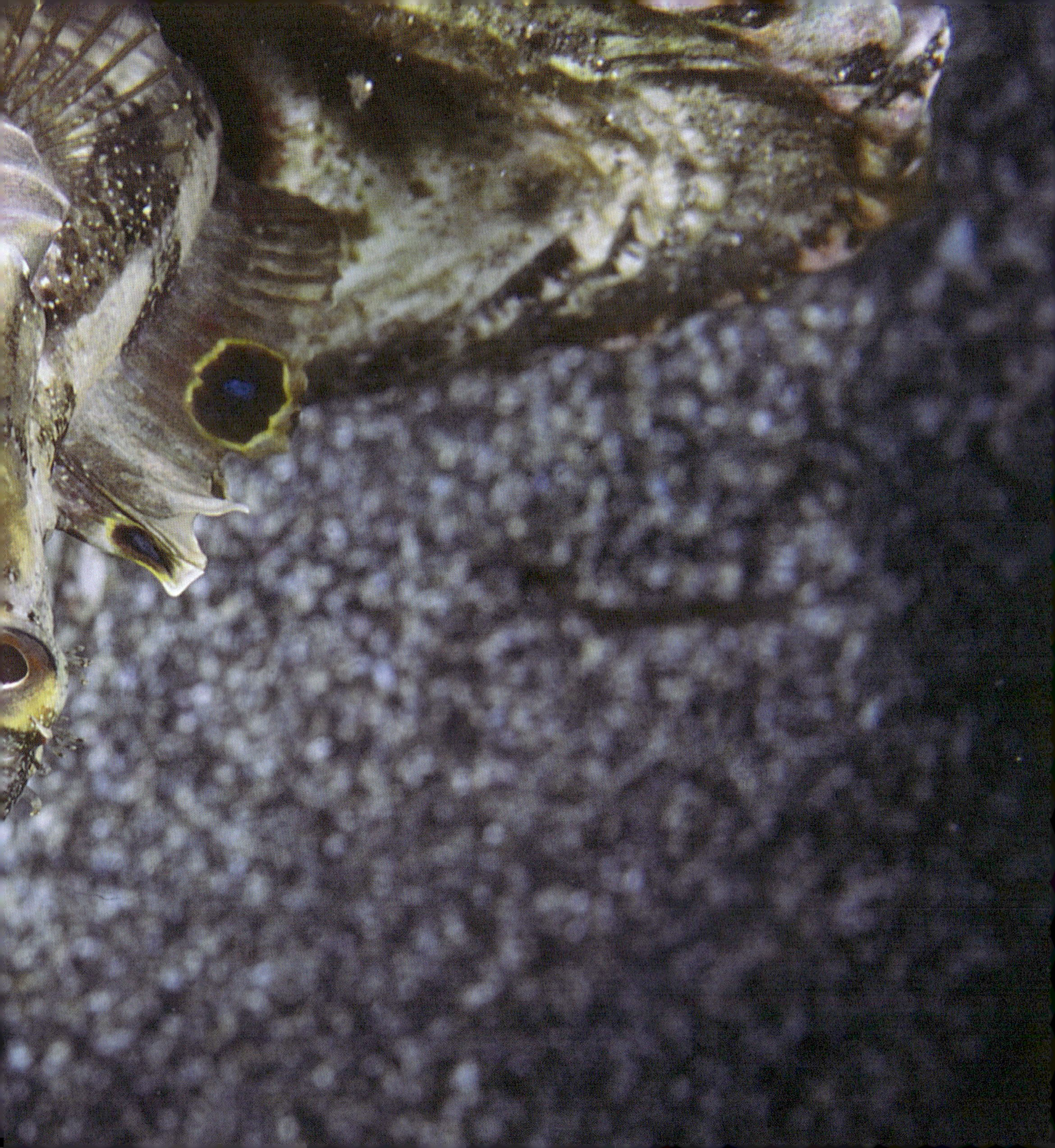

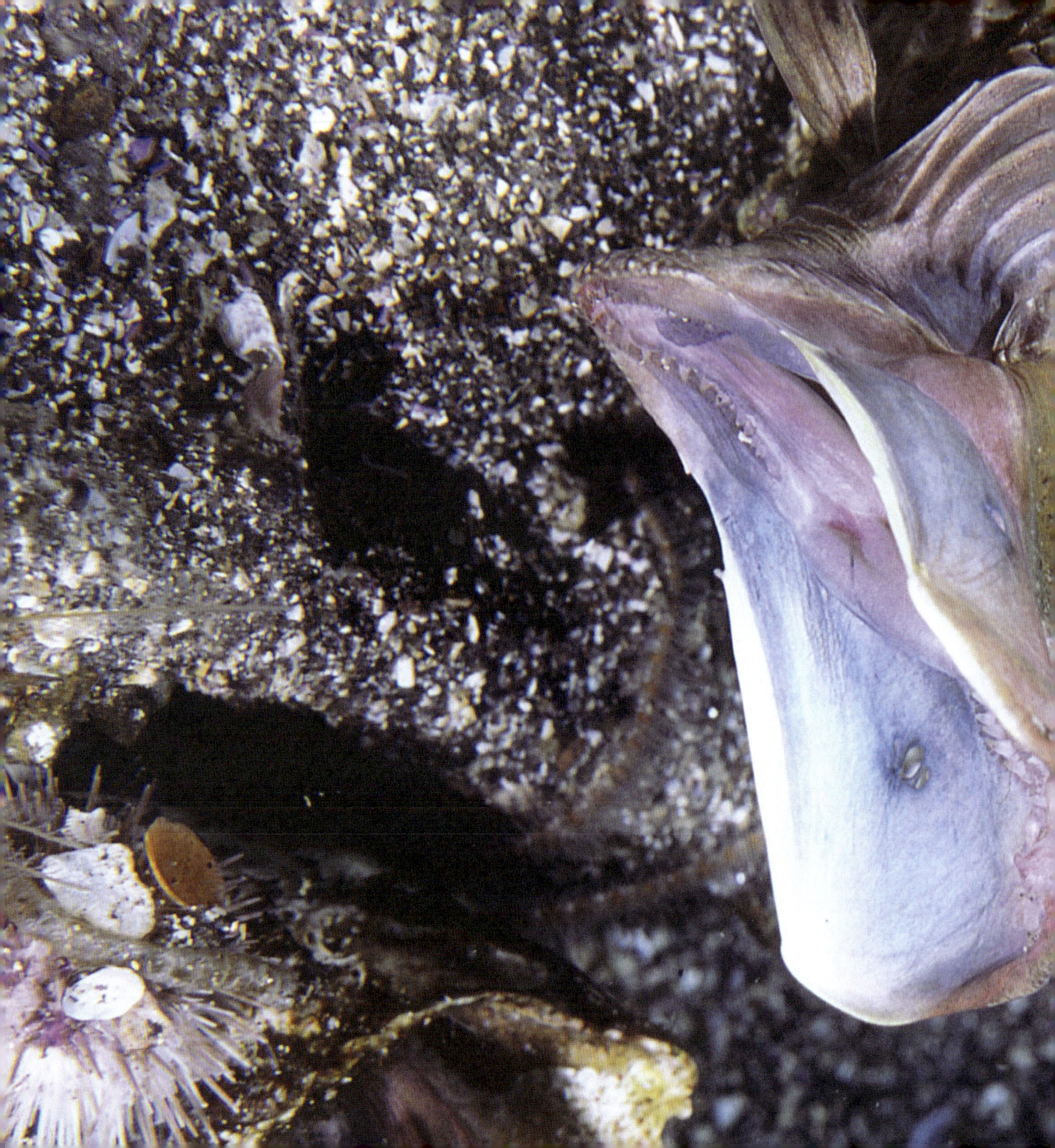

WOBBEGONG CARPET SHARK

spend much of their time resting on the sea floor. They are mostly found in shallow waters around Australia and Indonesia.

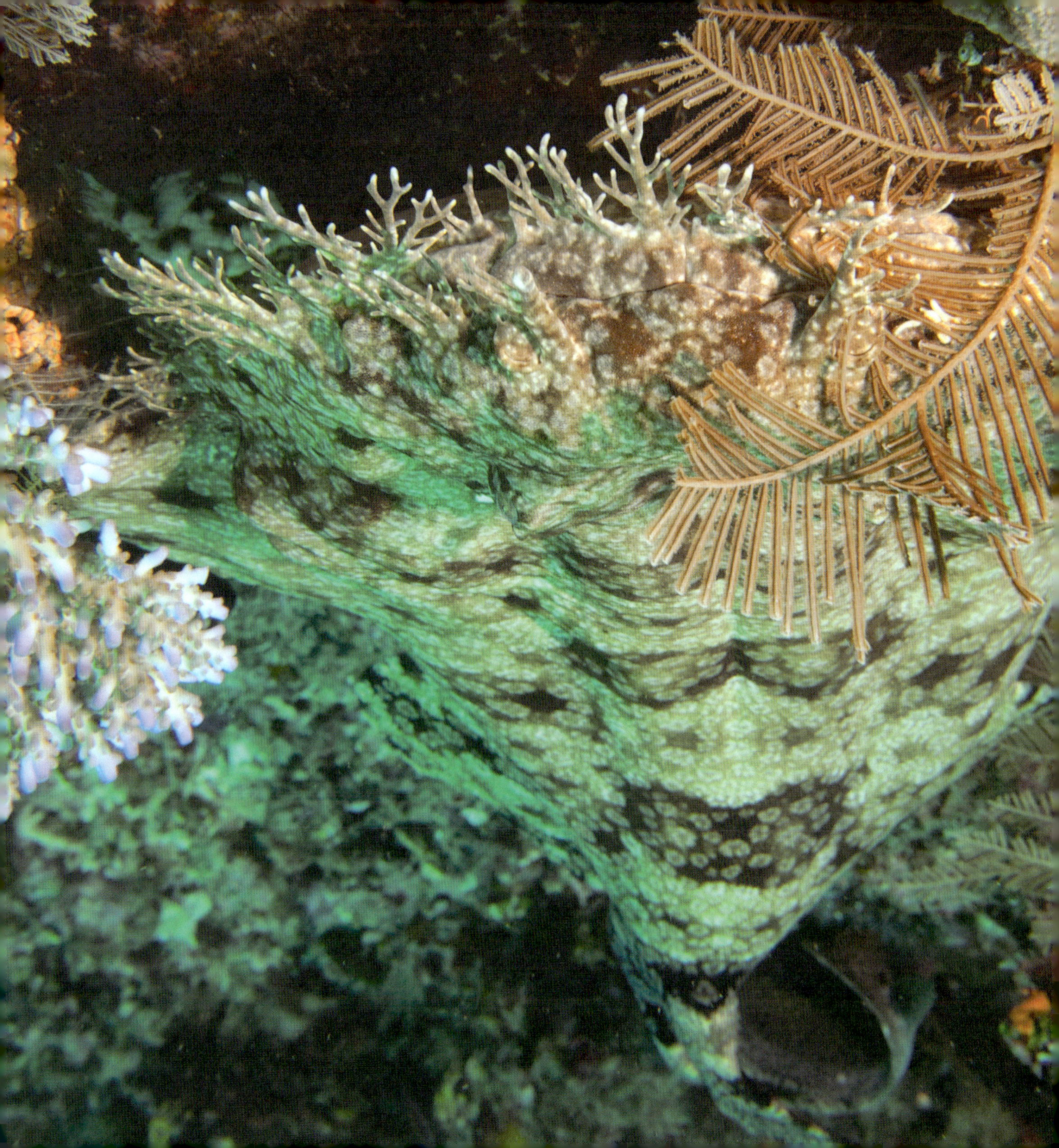

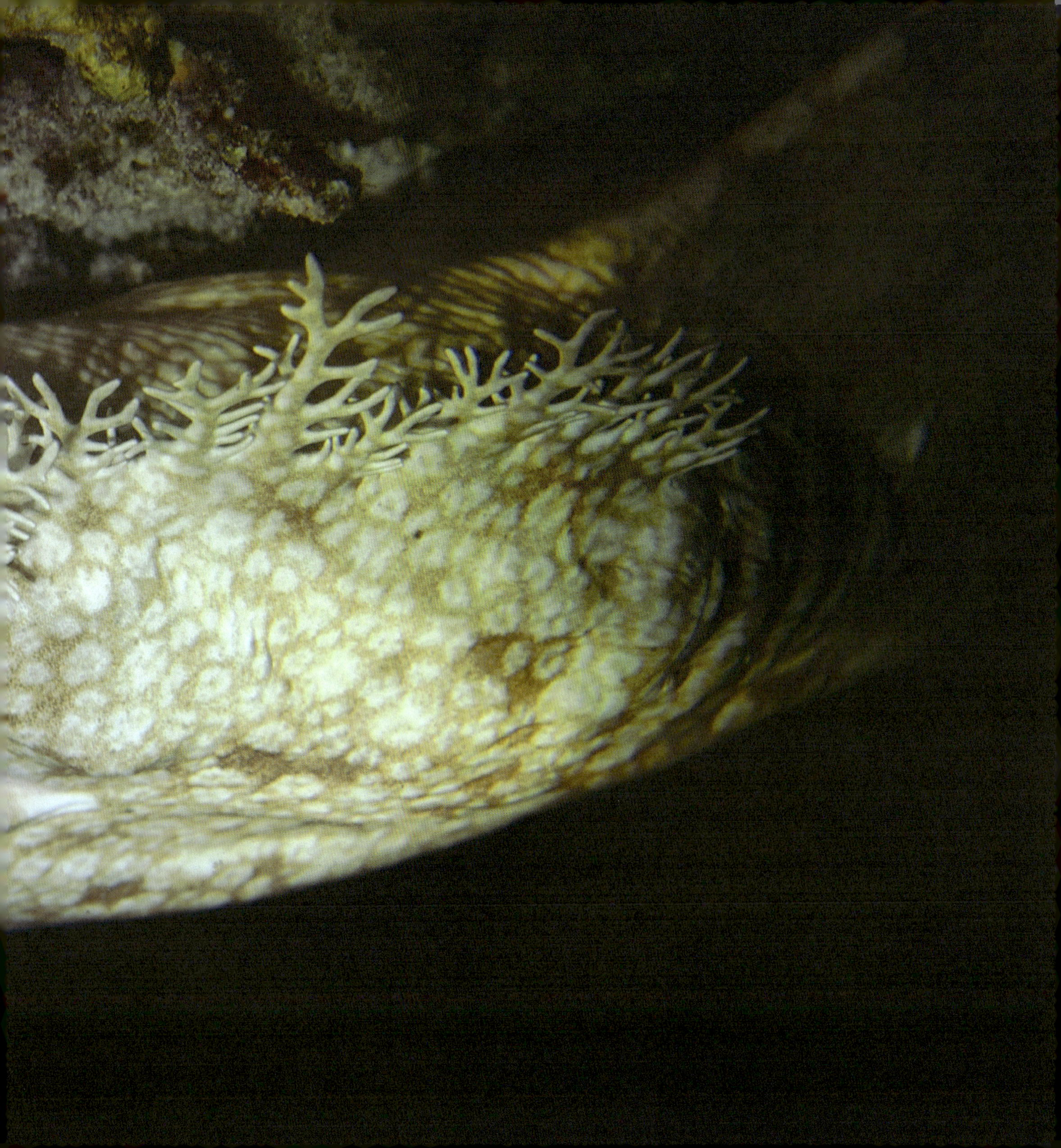

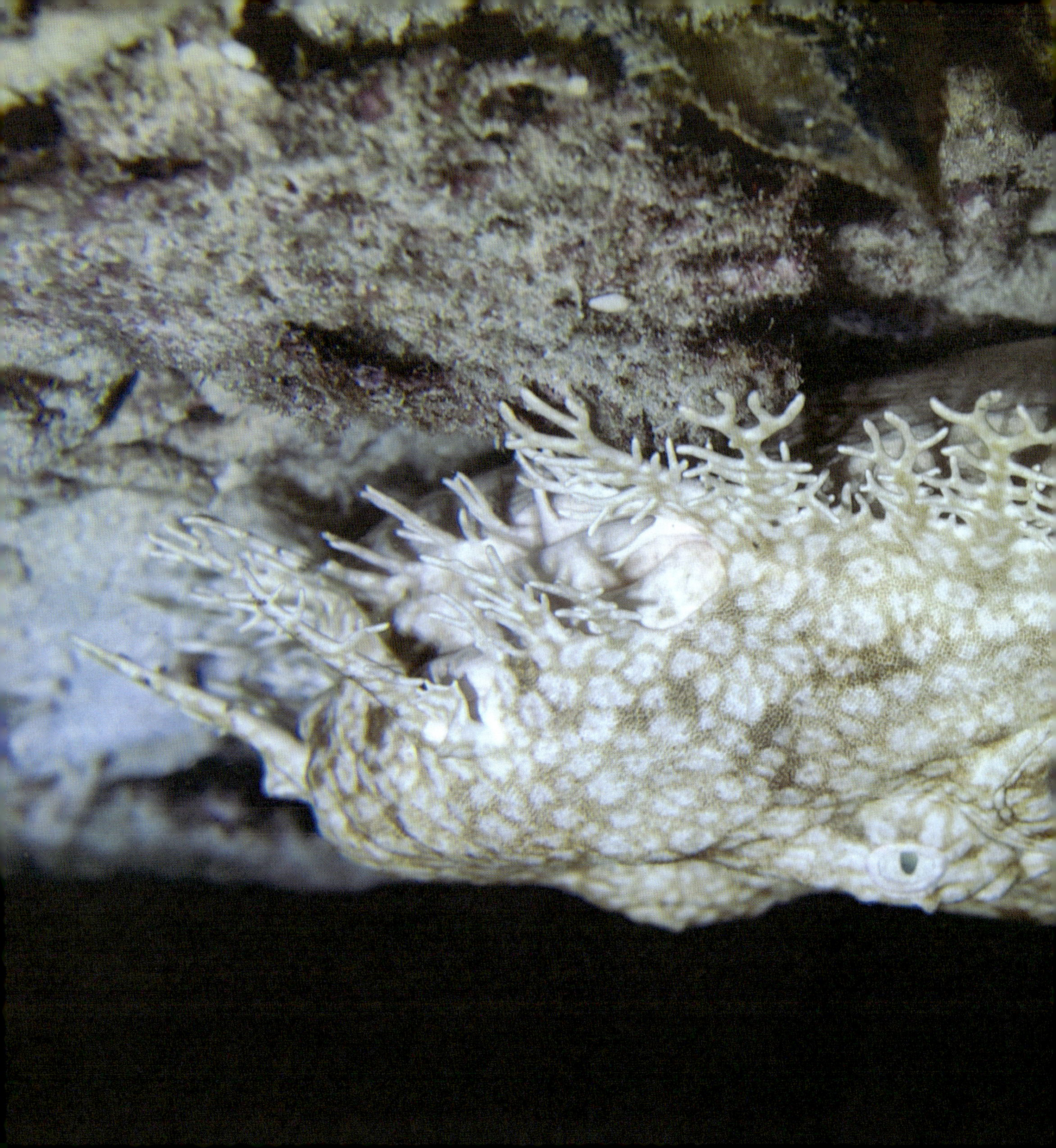

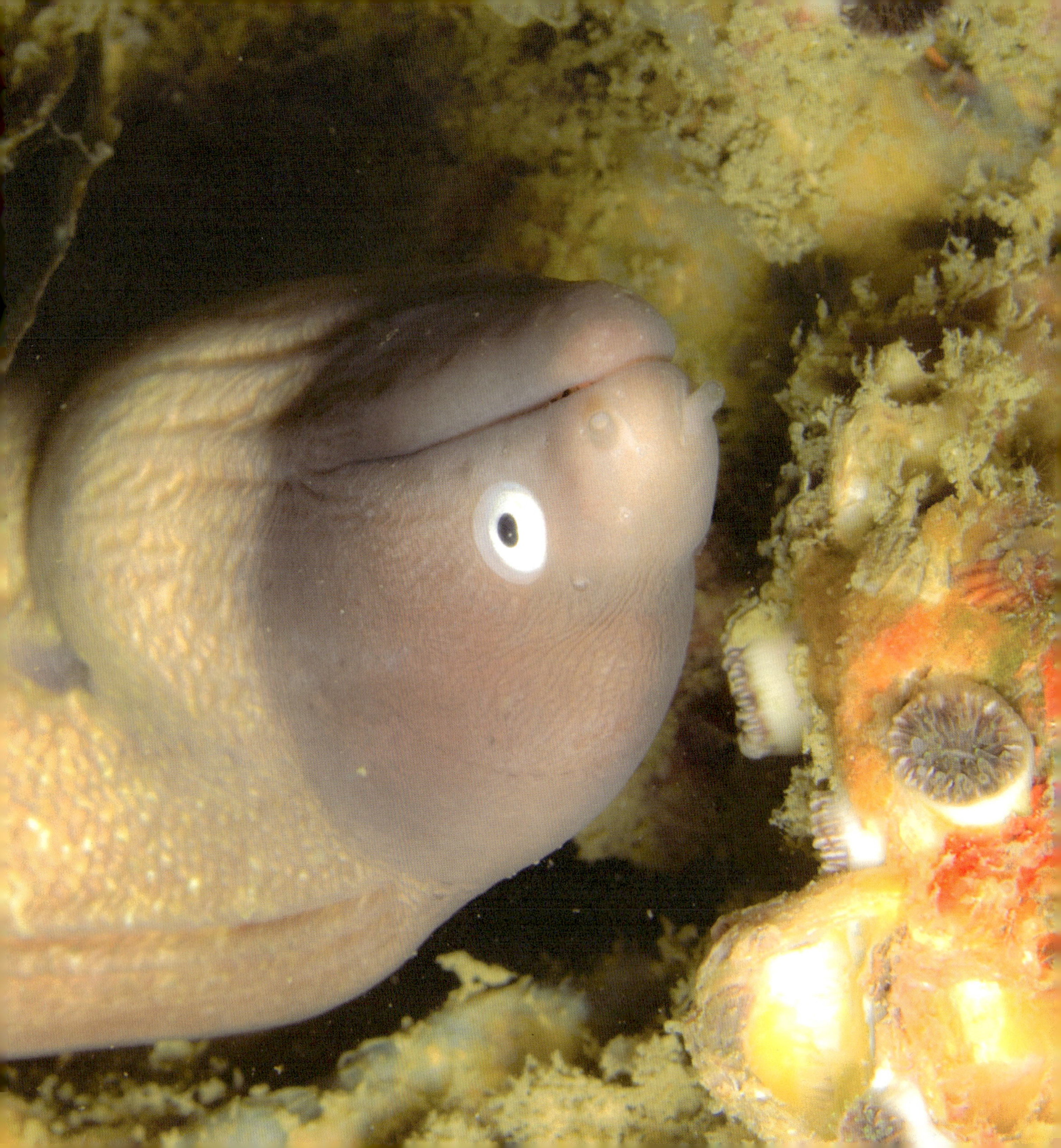

MORAY EEL

is the largest type of eel. Moray eel spends most of its time hidden in the caves on the bottom of the sea. Moray eel has a long and slender body which resembles to snake.

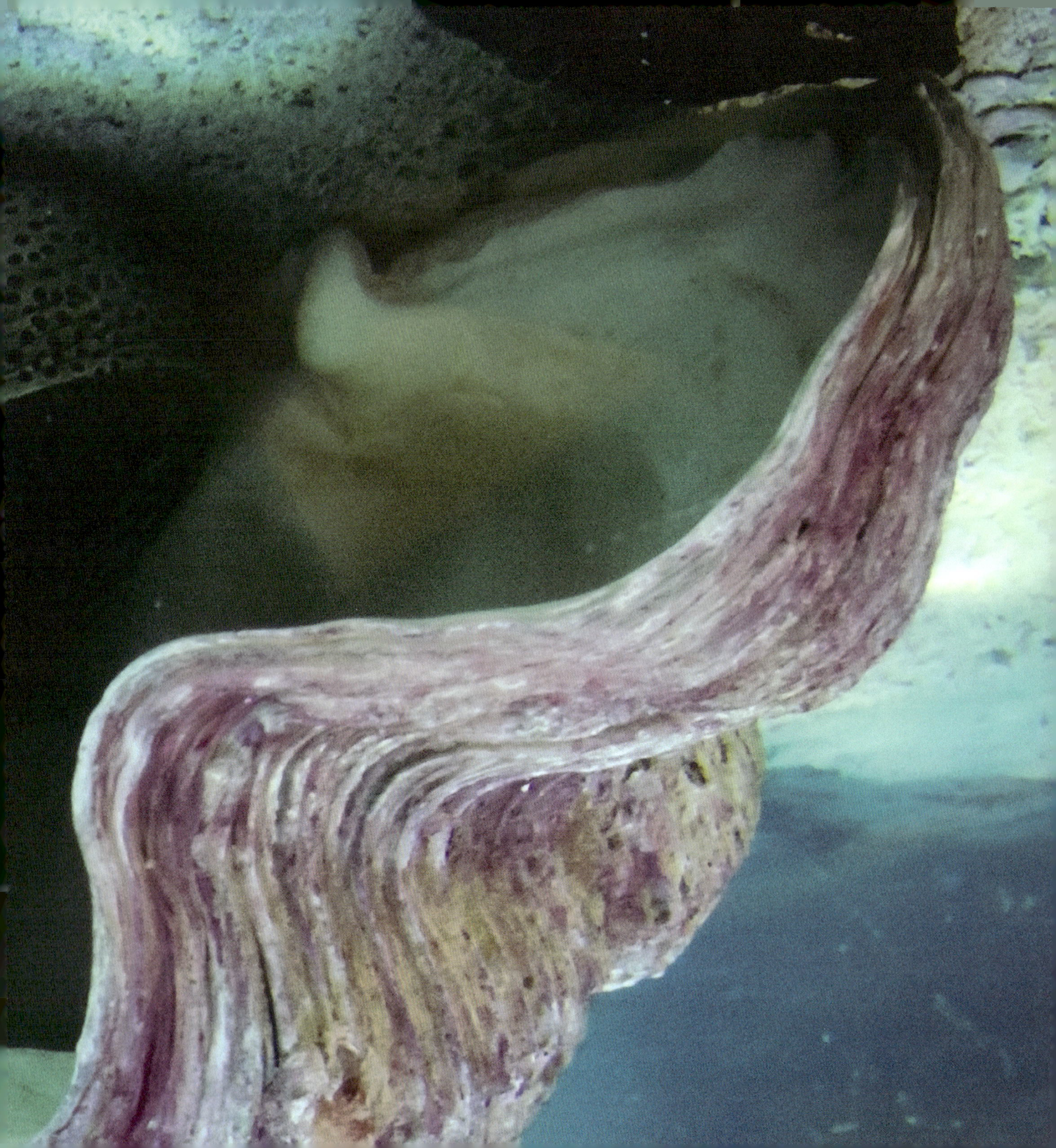

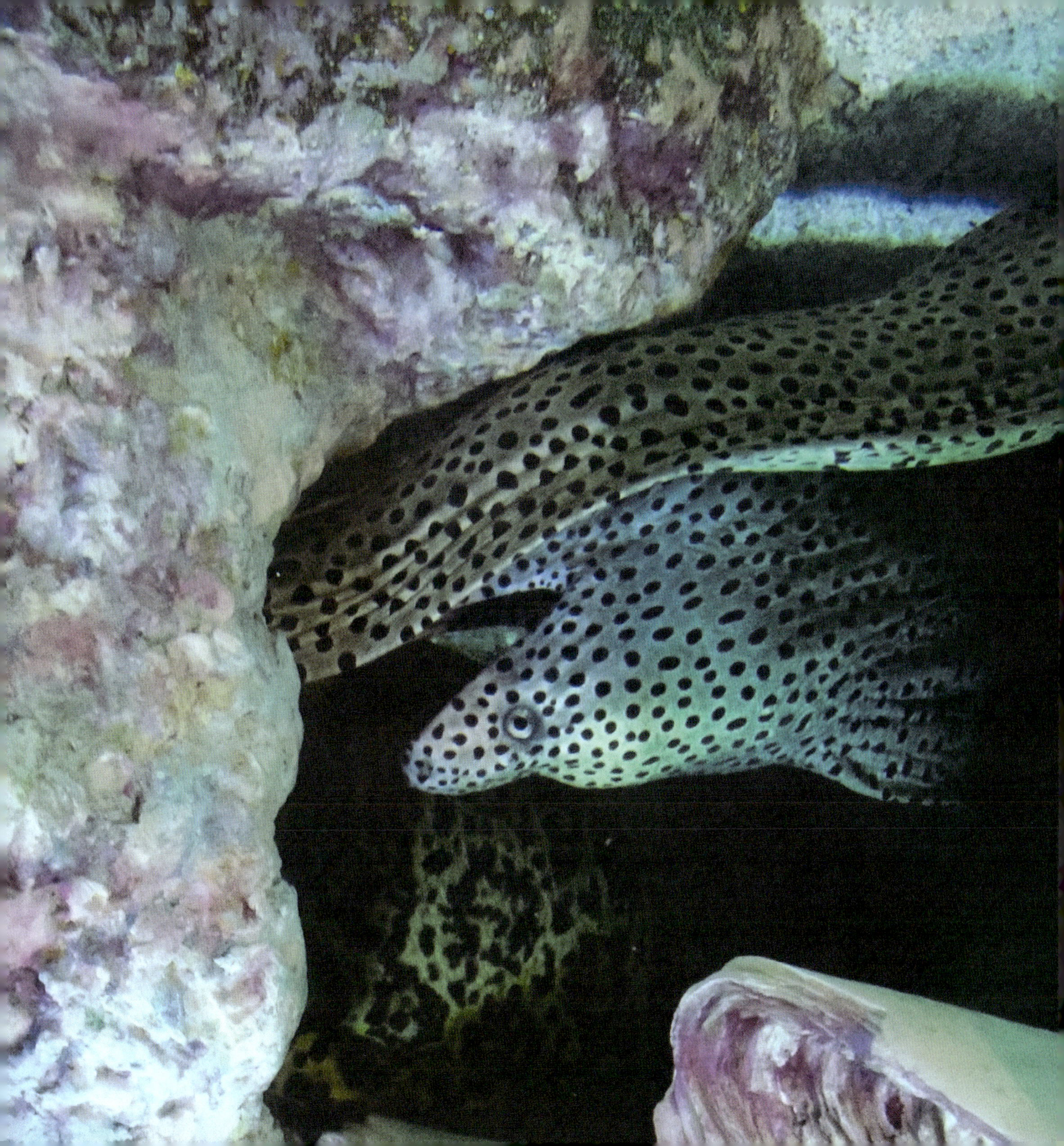

Printed in Great Britain
by Amazon